TO LOSE ONE'S SOUL

Exposing the Apostasy of the Religious Right

George Chumney

TO LOSE ONE'S SOUL

Exposing the Apostasy of the Religious Right

by George Chumney

Copyright ©2022 by George Chumney

ISBN: 9798985228601

BORGO
PUBLISHING

Tuscaloosa, Alabama
borgopublishing.com

Biblical quotations are from the New Revised Standard Version of the Bible, copyright ©1989, by the Division of Christian Education of the National Council of Churches of Christ in the United States of America. Used by permission. All rights reserved.

For Susan

[T]hose who say that religion has nothing to do with politics
do not know what religion means.

—MOHANDAS K. GANDHI, *AUTOBIOGRAPHY*

CONTENTS

PREFACE

THE IDEA FOR THIS BOOK FIRST OCCURRED TO ME IN 2019. LIKE millions of Americans, I had found it shocking that a contemptible individual like Donald Trump could win a presidential election with the overwhelming support of frequent churchgoers. So, during his third year in office, I thought about writing a series of scriptural meditations that would draw attention to the absurdity of Bible-believing Christians putting their faith in a man whose pronouncements and policies constantly contradicted the teaching of Jesus. My intention was to publish such a volume prior to the 2020 election. The coronavirus pandemic shifted my energies to other matters, and the election of Joe Biden gave me hope that there would no longer be any need for the sort of musings that I had envisioned.

That hope was dashed when it became apparent that Trump would not have the decency to fade into obscurity. Then came new inspiration. I discovered John Lithgow's brilliant trilogy of satirical poems splendidly skewering the man whom he aptly christened "Dumpty."[1] Lithgow's lyric lampooning of Trump encouraged me to reconsider my earlier plan. I realized that it is never too late to say something that needs to be said and that these brief biblical meditations might finally make a few people rethink their messianic devotion to a dangerous despot. Where Lithgow used

---

1   John Lithgow, *Dumpty: The Age of Trump in Verse* (San Francisco: Chronicle Prism, 2019); John Lithgow, *Trumpty Dumpty Wanted a Crown: Verses for a Despotic Age* (San Francisco: Chronicle Prism, 2020; John Lithgow, *A Confederacy of Dumptys: Portraits of American Scoundrels in Verse* (San Francisco: Chronicle Prism, 2021).

irreverent humor to offer a few moments of risible respite to Trump's discouraged opponents, I have relied on serious readings of Scripture to challenge Trump's ardent supporters to rethink their perspective and to reorient their lives.

I am a retired Presbyterian minister. During my years in the pulpit, I followed the counsel of Karl Barth, a theologian who advised members of the clergy to "take your Bible and take your newspaper and read both. But interpret newspapers from your Bible."[2] Nowadays, one's "newspaper" includes a broad range of media sources, and analysis of voting patterns in the last two presidential elections suggests that millions of churchgoers are listening to preachers whose interpretations of the Bible rely heavily on what they hear from right-wing media outlets. Indeed, because people in the pews spend so many hours listening to those same right-wing pundits, what preachers say may no longer register. I have written these twenty-four biblical meditations with such individuals in mind.

Writers have found it difficult to identify this demographic consistently, and I have not attempted to make well-defined theological distinctions either. Instead, I have adopted the terminology commonly found in the news media and polling research. I direct my concerns primarily to churchgoers who voted for Trump, Christians that pollsters have classified as white evangelicals and white Catholics and that media commentators have designated as the Religious Right. I hope that a few of these folks will find themselves moved by what I have written and that they in turn will challenge their peers to acknowledge the disparity between the faith that they profess and the political views that they espouse. I also encourage opponents of Trump to use these reflections to confront the hypocrisy of friends and family

2 "Barth in Retirement," 31 May 1963, content.time.com.

members who support him. Adult Bible study groups can use these meditations as a basis for discussion, and preachers can use them as the starting point for a couple of dozen sermons. So, there is something here for everyone.

Each of these meditations begins with a biblical text drawn from the New Revised Standard Version, and each briefly introduces readers to the original context of that passage. Readers who reject the methods of critical scholarship are free to ignore such historical and literary findings. If they want to believe that the story of Jonah recounts factual events or that King Solomon wrote Ecclesiastes, such beliefs will not undermine the import of the passage in question. In a few instances, I quibble with the way that the NRSV has rendered a particular word, offering what I consider a more suitable translation. I have used the footnotes to document quotations from public figures as well as factual assertions about contemporary events. Most churchgoers will be familiar with the biblical people, places, and events mentioned here. If they have any questions about such matters, they can consult a good Study Bible.

The title of this book uses strong language to characterize what I consider one of the most dangerous problems facing America today, and so I make no apologies for that choice of terms. In recent years, members of the Religious Right have gained unprecedented access to the corridors of power, but at great cost. Therefore, this book asks them the same question that Jesus asked his earliest followers: What will it profit you if you gain the whole world but forfeit your soul?

PROLOGUE

RECALL THE MOVIE *A FEW GOOD MEN*. THAT 1992 FILM STARS Tom Cruise, Jack Nicholson, and Demi Moore. Based on an Aaron Sorkin play first produced on Broadway three years earlier, this legal drama tells the story of a team of military lawyers assigned to defend two United States Marines accused of murder. In preparing for the court martial, the lawyers uncover evidence of a conspiracy that could exonerate their clients—if they can prove it.

Lance Corporal Harold Dawson and Private Louden Downey stand accused of murdering fellow Marine William Santiago at the Guantanamo Bay Naval Base in Cuba. Important questions remain, but undisputed evidence supports the charge. The case file shows that, prior to his death, Santiago had gone outside the chain of command to request a transfer from the base. It also shows that, in exchange for a transfer, he had offered to reveal the name of a fellow Marine who illegally fired his weapon across the fence line into Cuban territory. Even though Dawson and Downey admit that they bound Santiago, stuffed a rag into his mouth, and roughed him up to teach him a lesson, they insist that they never meant to kill him. Still, despite the tragic consequences of their actions, they also believe that they have done nothing wrong, because they have remained true to the Marine's code of honor: "Unit, Corps, God, and Country." An autopsy suggests that the probable cause of Santiago's death was an undetected toxin on the rag stuffed into his mouth; moreover, records indicate that it was Dawson who fired across the fence line, suggesting that he had an obvious motive for wanting to silence Santiago. The prosecution's case appears ironclad.

The defense lawyers assigned to the case, all junior members of the Judge Advocate Generals Corps, have little litigation experience. Lieutenant Commander JoAnne Galloway, a legal investigator for Internal Affairs, has volunteered to defend Dawson and Downey because she suspects that Santiago's death resulted from a botched "Code Red," an illegal hazing practice commonly conducted by enlisted personnel against one of their own to enforce discipline. Her superiors reluctantly make her part of the defense team but give the assignment of lead counsel to Lieutenant Daniel Kaffee, a lawyer with a reputation for avoiding the courtroom as often as possible by accepting plea bargains for his clients. The third member of the defense teams is Kaffee's friend and colleague Lieutenant Sam Weinburg. When Galloway shares the results of the preliminary investigation with Kaffee and Weinburg, she explains her theory that Dawson and Downey conducted a Code Red against Santiago but had no intention of killing him. Given the strength of the prosecution's case and the likelihood of his clients' conviction, Kaffee, true to form, focuses on securing the most favorable plea agreement possible.

Subsequent events, though, encourage Kaffee to reconsider matters. In his initial meeting with Dawson and Downey, the defendants confirm that Galloway's theory is correct: Santiago's death was the result of a Code Red gone wrong. Kaffee next meets with the prosecutor, Marine Captain Jack Ross, who unexpectedly offers to reduce the charges to avoid a trial. When asked what he knows about Code Reds, Ross sidesteps the question, telling Kaffee that, prior to the incident, Company Commander Lieutenant Kendrick had held a meeting with the entire unit and ordered them not to touch Santiago. Although Dawson confirms that account, he claims that Kendrick later came to his room and ordered the Code Red. On the defense team's visit to Guantanamo, Base Commander Colonel Nathan Jessup claims that he had authorized Santiago's transfer, but an inspection of Santiago's quarters shows that he had not packed his gear for the scheduled flight out. Galloway asks Jessup what he knows about Code Reds. He says that, on the record, he discourages the practice, but that, if it happens without his knowledge, "So be it." Finally, Kaffee asks for a copy of Santiago's transfer order, a routine request that provokes Jessup's noticeable ire.

Once the court marital gets under way, Kaffee does his best to defend his clients, but a series of setbacks makes it unlikely that he can secure an acquittal for Dawson and Downey. His carefully rehearsed cross-examination of the base physician fails to shake the doctor's finding that the probable cause of Santiago's death was an undetected toxin on the rag stuffed into his mouth. Under oath, Lieutenant Kendrick flatly denies that he ordered Dawson and Downey to conduct a Code Red against Santiago. Finally, during the prosecutor's cross-examination of Private Downey, the prosecutor forces him to admit that he was not present when Kendrick allegedly gave the Code Red order to Corporal Dawson. As a result, the pivotal argument in Kaffee's case— the claim that Dawson and Downey were following a direct order to conduct a Code Red against Santiago, given to them by Lieutenant Kendrick—boils down to Dawson's word against Kendrick's. At this point, Kaffee no longer thinks it possible to exonerate his clients, but Galloway suggests one last tactic: put Colonel Jessup on the stand and press him to acknowledge that he himself ordered the Code Red.

When Colonel Jessup takes the stand, Kaffee's initial line of questioning seems frivolous, but it does establish two pertinent facts. First, phone records show that Santiago never called anyone to share the news of his transfer. Second, the sealing of his room following his death shortly after midnight shows that he had not packed his gear for the scheduled 6:00 a.m. flight out. So, other than a written order, there is no evidence for Santiago's pending transfer. As Kaffee's line of questioning continues, Jessup unwittingly makes two conflicting claims. On the one hand, he confirms that he ordered Lieutenant Kendrick to prohibit his unit from harming Santiago. On the other hand, he maintains that he ordered Santiago's transfer because of the potential danger the young Marine faced from other members of his unit. Kaffee calls attention to the contradictory nature of those two orders: "If Kendrick gave an order that Santiago was not to be touched, then why did he have to be transferred?" As their increasingly belligerent exchanges continue, Kaffee asks Jessup directly, "Did you order the Code Red?" In the heat of the moment, without realizing the legal implications of his answer, Jessup angrily admits, "You're goddamn right I did!"

Even though the jury finds Corporal Dawson and Private Downey not guilty of murder, it does, nonetheless, find them guilty of conduct unbecoming a United States Marine, resulting in their dishonorable discharge. Because they were following orders, Downey does not understand the verdict, blurting out, "We did nothing wrong!" Dawson, however, knows better. "Yes, we did," he tells his friend. "We were supposed to fight for people who couldn't fight for themselves. We were supposed to fight for Willie [Santiago]."

Lieutenant Daniel Kaffee is the drama's protagonist. Early scenes establish that he is not truly invested either in the military or in the legal profession. In every situation, he does only enough to get by. He invariably follows the path of least resistance, as evidenced by the forty-four plea bargains that comprise his entire record as a defense attorney. He shows no interest in pursuing justice for his clients. He only wants to finish his required term of service in the United States

Navy so that he can move on to a more lucrative career in the private sector. Yet, in this instance, fate intervenes. Kaffee's clients reject any discussion of a plea deal, thereby forcing him to mount a serious defense. His colleagues provide the support he needs, and together they build the strongest case possible. For the first time in his career, Kaffee fulfills his potential, embraces his responsibility, and does his job. He pursues the truth, even when that means putting his own career in jeopardy. In the end, he finds himself transformed by the experience. He has earned the respect of both his colleagues and his clients. He has proven himself a gifted litigator, but, perhaps more importantly, he has also proven himself to be a good person.

The drama's denouement reveals that Lance Corporal Harold Dawson, too, finds himself transformed by this experience. From the moment that he obeyed Lieutenant Kendrick's order to conduct a Code Red against Private Santiago until the moment that the court announced its verdict, Dawson had convinced himself that he had done his duty, that he had upheld the Marine Corps' code of honor. Yet what he witnessed during the proceedings has forced him to reconsider what his duty required of him. In a moment of intellectual clarity, he sees that obeying an order from a superior officer can never be treated as a moral absolute. Instead, he recognizes that, by failing to protect a fellow Marine, he has betrayed his own integrity. Dawson's dishonorable discharge has cost him any chance of fulfilling a lifelong dream. Nevertheless, by confronting the truth and accepting its consequences, he has proven himself worthy of more respect than he could have ever received from wearing the uniform of a United States Marine. His exceptional courage provides a stark contrast to the empty bluster of men like Jessup and Kendrick, neither of whom will ever be half the man that Dawson has become.

The movie *A Few Good Men* addresses a range of themes, only one of which receives attention here—an individual's willingness to change. Many people need to make changes in their lives, but not everyone who needs to change does so. Sometimes, circumstances and events offer people a fresh perspective, and they take advantage of the opportunity to change, even when it involves making difficult choices. Of course, other people who confront those same circumstances and events go right on with their lives without a second thought. The Judeo-Christian tradition uses the word *repentance* to denote the sort of marked change that occurs in the life of Harold Dawson. In the biblical literature, repentance involves more than feeling remorse or regret; it requires a radical change of mind, one evidenced by a commensurate reordering of behavior. When the audience first sees Harold Dawson, he undoubtedly regrets what happened to William Santiago, but he has not yet come to grips with the depth of his own wrongdoing. However, by the time the movie ends, Dawson has experienced a moral awakening, one that has totally transformed his perspective and enabled him to begin moving in a whole new direction.

Most discussions about the nature of the Bible refer to one passage in particular; however, the folks who cite it usually focus all their attention on the idea of divine inspiration, without noticing what the passage has to say about the Bible's purpose and function: "All Scripture is...useful for teaching, for reproof, for correction, and for training in righteousness, so that everyone who belongs to God may be proficient, equipped for every good work" (2 Tim 3:16). The meditations that follow take very seriously the idea of using the Bible for reproof and correction. These brief reflections begin with a biblical text; then, based on that text, they show that the prevailing values, attitudes, and actions of America's Religious Right reflect precious little that is recognizably Christian. By directing attention to the practical implications of Scripture, these meditations provide members of the Religious Right an opportunity to repent—to rethink their perspective and to reorient their lives. Of course, not everyone who needs to change is willing to do so. While some on the Religious Right may summon the exceptional courage shown by Harold Dawson, others will remain content with the empty bluster of Nathan Jessup.

MEDITATION 1

If my people who are called by my name humble themselves,
pray, seek my face, and turn from their wicked ways,
then I will hear from heaven, and will forgive their sin
and heal their land.

—2 Chronicles 7:14

LIKE A HOST OF BIBLICAL TEXTS, 2 CHRONICLES 7:14 ENJOYS GREAT popularity with the Religious Right in America. In times of national crisis, they see the verse as a call to prayer, because they view whatever has befallen the country as a sign of divine judgment. Moreover, they point the finger of blame at their adversaries, the godless wrongdoers who must turn from their errant ways to avert further calamity.

In the aftermath of the terrorist attacks of September 11, televangelists Jerry Falwell and Pat Robertson maintained that an angry deity had withdrawn special protection from America because it had rejected their brand of Christian values. The blame for what had transpired, they said, lay with those who were trying to "secularize America."[1] In other words, we Christians need to pray that those folks repent before it is too late.

Maybe members of the Religious Right need to read the text more carefully. Nothing is said about two opposing factions, one that needs to pray and another that needs to change its ways. The deity addresses but one group, his people who are called by his name. If members of the Religious Right want to claim this verse and its promises, they must recognize that they themselves are the ones who must change their ways.

---

1 Laurie Goodstein, "After the Attacks: Finding Fault," 15 September 2001, nytimes.com.

The biblical text speaks of a process that begins with people humbling themselves, a step that members of the Religious Right nowadays seem loath to take. The long-coveted political power that they currently wield at both the state and national levels has encouraged hubris, not humility. They remain focused primarily on accruing power and projecting strength. To humble themselves in any way might suggest uncertainty or weakness.

In 2015, Donald Trump said that he had never sought divine forgiveness.[2] Pundits found that admission surprising because it contradicted what members of the Religious Right ostensibly wanted to hear. Once Trump was elected, with their overwhelming support,[3] their religious beliefs continued to have negligible impact on the policies that he pursued. Instead, members of the Religious Right demonstrated an increasing willingness to betray their beliefs by embracing, endorsing, or simply acquiescing to whatever Trump said or did.

Trump responded to the "Unite the Right" rally in 2017 by drawing a moral equivalency between the rally's white supremacist participants and counter-protesters who used the occasion to denounce racism.[4] Prominent leaders of the Religious Right such as Jerry Falwell, Jr., Franklin Graham, and Mike Huckabee refused to condemn the president's words, with Huckabee assuring reporters that Trump "has the faith community."[5] If the faith community calls "evil good and good evil" (Isa 5:20), what is the content of their faith?

---

2   Eugene Scott, "Trump Believes in God, but Hasn't Sought Forgiveness," 18 July 2015, cnn.com

3   Jessica Martínez and Gregory A. Smith, "How the Faithful Voted: A Preliminary 2016 Analysis," 9 November 2016, pewresearch.org.

4   Glenn Thrush and Maggie Haberman, "Trump Gives White Supremacists an Unequivocal Boost," 15 August 2017, nytimes.com.

5   Doina Chiacu and Sarah N. Lynch, "Prominent U.S. Religious Conservatives Defend Trump after Charlottesville," 20 August 2017, reuters.com.

MEDITATION 2

Remember this and consider, recall it to mind, you transgressors,
remember the former things of old;
for I am God, and there is no other;
I am God, and there is no one like me.
—Isaiah 46:8–9

The deity directs these stern words toward transgressors, people who have clearly broken the divine law. So, members of the Religious Right usually take for granted that a passage like this one applies to other folks, not them. Indeed, they see themselves as the ones who have consistently defended and upheld biblical principles. Too bad those other folks are not in church to hear this stinging rebuke.

Yet the divine injunction appeals to the listeners' memory, to their thoughtful consideration of matters concerning which they should need no reminder. In its original context, the reprimand is directed toward the people of Israel, not their pagan neighbors. It speaks directly and forcefully to people who claim to know the truth. Thus, in today's world, it has more to say to churchgoers than it does to unbelievers.

So, what is it that these people know all too well but have now apparently lost sight of? It is the most fundamental precept of their faith: the oneness and incomparability of the deity himself. Like the Israelites of old, Christians today look with scorn on people who bow down to graven images, but the Bible's concern with idolatry invariably focuses not on the primitive devotion of pagans but on the fickle duplicity of the faithful.

In the pages of Scripture, it is the members of the believing community who are censured for putting their trust in something or someone other than their creator, for wanting to hedge their bets, for attempting to "serve two masters" (Mt 6:24). They seem confident that they can compartmentalize life, that they can neatly separate personal religious beliefs from everyday public activities. Yet the integrity of reality belies that endeavor.

At the Republican National Convention in 2016, when Donald Trump accepted his party's nomination for president, he sketched a grim picture of what was wrong with America (in his view) and then offered a remedy. As columnist Yoni Appelbaum has observed, Trump broke with longstanding tradition by never acknowledging a need for help, whether human or divine. Instead, he claimed that he himself was America's only hope. He stated, "I alone can fix it."[1]

Trump portrayed himself as godlike, saying, in effect, "There is no one like me." In their lust for political influence, members of the Religious Right applauded that claim and placed their trust in a vulgar, racist megalomaniac. People who had once proclaimed a commitment to family values now embraced a man who exhibited contempt for any ethical standard. Already little more than a dependable voting bloc, the Religious Right opted to become a cult.

Members of the Religious Right have traded the birthright of their faith for fleeting political power. They have made a Faustian bargain with an opportunistic demagogue. His rhetoric is blasphemy, their devotion, idolatry.

---

1   Yoni Appelbaum, "I Alone Can Fix It," 21 July 2016, theatlantic.com.

MEDITATION 3

There are six things that the LORD *hates,*
seven that are an abomination to him:
haughty eyes, a lying tongue, and hands that shed innocent blood,
a heart that devises wicked plans, feet that hurry to run to evil,
a lying witness who testifies falsely,
and one who sows discord in a family.
—PROVERBS 6:16–19

ASCRIBING CULPABLE AGENCY TO VARIOUS PARTS OF THE BODY, THE biblical writer enumerates human inclinations that the deity finds abhorrent. In each case, the result involves the destructive use of a God-given ability. Because such conduct ordinarily elicits universal condemnation, it might seem unthinkable that people who profess to uphold biblical values would ignore or excuse that behavior. Yet that is what the Religious Right routinely chooses to do.

From Donald Trump's first day in office, he repeatedly lied to the American public. Some falsehoods remained innocuous, like his claims about the size of the crowd at his inauguration.[1] Other lies, however, proved lethal and far-reaching, like his deliberate deception about the threat posed by the coronavirus.[2] As corpses piled up outside hospitals, Americans looked to Trump for empathy, but their distress was met only with the haughty gaze of indifference.

Make no mistake, Donald Trump has innocent blood on his hands. Infectious disease experts maintain that the U.S.

---

1   Julie Hirschfeld Davis and Matthew Rosenberg, "With False Claims, Trump Attacks Media on Turnout and Intelligence Rifts," 21 January 2017, nytimes.com.
2   Rachel Martin and Steve Inskeep, "Trump Tells Woodward He Deliberately Downplayed Coronavirus Threat," 10 September 2020, npr.org.

death toll resulting from the coronavirus would have been significantly lower but for Trump's irresponsible leadership.[3] Of course, Republican governors who followed his lead by refusing to take public health precautions against the pandemic share responsibility for those unnecessary deaths, as do their supporters.

Donald Trump, the man who had campaigned on a platform of "America First," prioritized his own personal interests above the common good. If that was not evident from his mishandling of the pandemic, it became obvious during the weeks following the 2020 election. Like a petulant toddler who cannot accept losing a game, he responded to his election defeat by insisting that others must have cheated.

At Trump's insistence, his lawyers alleged that the presidential election had been stolen through voter fraud, but the result of more than sixty cases filed in state or federal courts was the same: neither the facts nor the law supported those allegations.[4] Nonetheless, Trump continued to pursue illicit schemes to overturn the election, efforts that culminated on January 6, 2021, when he incited his supporters' violent attack on the Capitol.[5]

Since Donald Trump entered the political arena, he has embodied the very impulses and inclinations that the Scriptures condemn. Yet members of the Religious Right have responded not by repudiating his attitudes and actions but by giving him their unwavering support. The fork in the road now lies behind them; they have chosen the way of apostasy.

---

3 Amy B. Wang, "Birx Tells CNN 'Most U.S. Deaths Could Have Been Mitigated' after First 100,000," 27 March 2021, washingtonpost.com.
4 Jim Rutenberg, Nick Corasaniti, and Alan Feuer, "Trump's Fraud Claim Died in Court, but the Myth of Stolen Elections Lives On," 11 October 2021, nytimes.com.
5 David Leonhardt, "Rampage at the Capitol," 7 January 2021, nytimes.com.

MEDITATION 4

For my thoughts are not your thoughts,
nor are your ways my ways, says the LORD.
For as the heavens are higher than the earth,
so are my ways higher than your ways
and my thoughts than your thoughts.

—ISAIAH 55:8–9

THE PROPHET, PRIVY TO DIVINE REVELATION, DRAWS A DISTINCTION between the ideas and actions of the deity and those of his audience. In its original context, these words reference their immediate circumstances—a momentous turn of events, something previously unimaginable. A generation before theirs had witnessed the destruction of Jerusalem and the exile of its people, but that divine judgment now culminates in restoration and rebuilding.

In one sense, of course, these words look back to another world, what for today's readers is ancient history. Yet, for those who identify as Christians, these words are a part of sacred Scripture and can, through interpretation, continue to have normative relevance. So, what might be the significance of these words to churchgoers in the United States in the twenty-first century? Does the distinction described still hold true?

When people get an eye exam, the eye care professional asks them to look at an eye chart through a device known as a phoropter. As the technician changes lenses, the patient gives subjective feedback about which settings provide better vision: Which is clearer, A or B? In the same way, people can make a subjective judgment about which of two distinct scenarios more nearly approximates the ways and thoughts of the deity.

7

In the Declaration of Independence, Thomas Jefferson made this unequivocal statement: "We hold these truths to be self-evident: that all men are created equal."[1] Less than a decade later, in *Notes on the State of Virginia*, he said, "I advance it therefore as a suspicion only, that the blacks, whether originally a distinct race, or made distinct by time and circumstances, are inferior to whites in the endowments of both body and mind."[2]

Even though those two utterances are obviously contradictory, they do reflect the divergent opinions held by most white people living in America at that time. So, it seems entirely fair to ask members of today's Religious Right, which of those two views more nearly approximates the thoughts of the biblical deity, A or B?

Now consider a contemporary example, the voter-suppression measures enacted by state legislatures following the Supreme Court's decision to invalidate a key part of the Voting Rights Act of 1965.[3] These laws have closed polling places and created stricter voting ID laws, ostensibly to prevent voter fraud. In fact, such legislation addresses a problem that does not exist and invariably has a disproportionate impact on voters of color.[4]

In terms of partisan politics, such measures deliberately benefit the Republican party, the group solely responsible for their passage. In terms of social justice, however, they disenfranchise citizens in the same way that Jim Crow laws once did. So it seems entirely fair to ask members of today's Religious Right, do these discriminatory measures approximate the ways of the biblical deity?

---

1 The Declaration of Independence, in *Thomas Jefferson: Writings* (New York: Library of America, 1984), 19
2 Thomas Jefferson, *Notes on the State of Virginia*, Query XIV, in *Thomas Jefferson: Writings* (New York: Library of America, 1984), 270.
3 *Shelby County v. Holder*, 570 U.S. 529 (2013).
4 P. R. Lockhart, "How *Shelby County v. Holder* Upended Voting Rights in America," 25 June 2019, vox.com

MEDITATION 5

Jesus said to them, "Isaiah prophesied rightly about you hypocrites,
as it is written, 'This people honors me with their lips,
but their hearts are far from me;
in vain do they worship me, teaching human precepts as doctrines.'
You abandon the commandment of God
and hold to human tradition."

—MARK 7:6–8

WHEN RIVALS QUESTION HIS DISCIPLES' CONDUCT, JESUS REBUFFS their presumptuous attack, citing scathing words from the prophet Isaiah against them. That denunciation reframes the debate by challenging the integrity of Jesus' opponents. The disparity between their professed beliefs and everyday actions betrays the true content of their character. By routinely ignoring, even blatantly defying, Torah's dictates concerning justice, they prove themselves pious frauds.

New Testament scholars often raise concerns about the gospels' tendency to caricature the various antagonists of Jesus, as though they were all holier-than-thou hypocrites. Nevertheless, the insidious proclivities censured here are commonly observed. Most people have encountered folks who adopt such a stance, whether individually or as a group. Thus, the problem addressed here is real, justifying the words spoken by Jesus, and by Isaiah before him.

As historian Randall Balmer shows in his book *Bad Faith*, the most glaring contemporary example of the hypocrisy that Jesus condemns is the Religious Right.[1] Ostensibly founded to restore Christian values to the public square,

---

1 Randall Balmer, *Bad Faith: Race and the Rise of the Religious Right* (Grand Rapids: Eerdmans, 2021).

this group has become little more than an unholy alliance of white evangelicals and white Catholics, hell-bent on maintaining white supremacy in American society.

Balmer demonstrates that the true catalyst for the Religious Right was not the Supreme Court's legalization of abortion.[2] Instead, it was a U.S. District Court's decision two years earlier that denied Federal tax exemptions to racially discriminatory private schools.[3] White Christians mobilized immediately to defend racial segregation. Opposition to abortion was only added to their agenda years later, in part to deflect attention from their racist policies.[4]

Members of the Religious Right profess to acknowledge as Lord one who emphasized the biblical injunction to "love your neighbor as yourself" (Lev 19:18: Mk 12:31), with no proviso about the color of the neighbor's skin. Yet they have repeatedly abandoned that divine mandate when it conflicts with their cherished tradition of white supremacy. Paraphrasing James Baldwin, Jesus might conclude, "I cannot believe what they say, because I see what they do."[5]

---

2 *Roe v. Wade*, 410 U.S. 113 (1973).
3 *Green v. Connally*, 330 F. Supp. 1150 (D.D.C. 1971).
4 Balmer, *Bad Faith*, 64–65.
5 James Baldwin, "A Report from Occupied Territory," in *Collected Essays*, ed. Toni Morrison (New York: Library of America, 1998), 738.

MEDITATION 6

So God created humankind in his image,
in the image of God he created them;
male and female he created them.

—Genesis 1:27

An omniscient narrator reports the fashioning of humanity, male and female, in what is termed the deity's "image." Although theological debate continues concerning precisely what the divine image denotes, most interpreters agree that in this context it includes humankind's responsibility to govern the natural order as a steward, accountable to the creator. The phrase would also seem to imply the sanctity of human life.

The Religious Right's opposition to abortion invariably appeals to this passage—though, as previously noted, that stance only solidified after savvy political operatives observed that the so-called pro-life agenda resonated with voters already galvanized by their commitment to racial segregation.[1] Still, the portrayal of a fetus as a human being bearing the divine image might seem to some people a not-implausible religious rationale for opposing abortion.

The strength of that argument is, paradoxically, also its weakness. The Religious Right has shown little interest in children's well-being (after birth). Even as its members insist that the government deny a woman's right to choose, they demand further funding cuts for public programs designed to provide adequate food, shelter, and medical care for needy children.[1] The inconsistency of these morally irreconcilable actions is damning.

---

1 Randall Balmer, *Bad Faith: Race and the Rise of the Religious Right* (Grand Rapids: Eerdmans, 2021), 38–49.

11

When Donald Trump branded Mexican immigrants as "rapists" and "criminals,"[2] no outcry ensued from members of the Religious Right about these individuals being human beings created in the divine image. Instead, they applauded his xenophobic rhetoric. When Trump asked why the United States still accepted refugees from "shithole countries," members of the Religious Right endorsed that sentiment, only decrying his vulgar language.[3]

Like so many biblical texts, Genesis 1:27 enjoys great popularity with America's Religious Right, but only when it seems to support a partisan position they have already adopted for more worldly reasons. In the debate about abortion, for example, they are quick to use the passage as a cudgel against their adversaries. Yet the teaching that human beings are created in the divine image clearly has no other meaningful role in shaping their core political views.

---

2   Daniel Victor, "Donald Trump's Lousy Week (Except for the Polling)," 2 July 2015, nytimes.com.
3   Sarah Pulliam Bailey, "Trump's 'Shithole' Comments Have Enraged Many, But Some Evangelical Leaders Still Back Him," 12 January 2018, washingtonpost.com.

MEDITATION 7

You shall not take vengeance or bear a grudge against any of your people, but you shall love your neighbor as yourself: I am the LORD.
—LEVITICUS 19:18

IN ITS ORIGINAL HISTORICAL CONTEXT, THIS INJUNCTION HAS limited application. The word *neighbor* refers solely to a fellow Israelite, while the word *love* denotes the understanding and forgiveness that one would want to receive in a case of one's own personal wrongdoing. Over time, however, both the Jewish and Christian traditions have generalized this mandate, regarding it as a concise summary of all the Torah's ethical expectations.

A careful reading of the gospels leaves no doubt that Jesus bases much of his teaching on this text. Indeed, he maintains that this demand should take precedence over all others save one, the imperative that one give one's ultimate devotion to the deity alone (Mk 12:31). Likewise, Jesus rejects the conventional restrictions on the word *neighbor*. He insists that one's neighbor is anyone in need, including one's enemy (Lk 10:25–37; Mt 5:43–48).

When one examines the priorities on which members of the Religious Right have focused their attention, one sees little indication that this fundamental mandate has had any meaningful impact on their public positions. Despite Jesus' emphasis on loving one's neighbor and his radical expansion of what that entails, much of what one finds on the Religious Right's agenda nowadays directly contradicts his teaching.

13

In 2012, a Colorado baker refused to provide a cake for a same-sex couple's wedding reception.[1] In 2013, a Virgina school board refused to allow a transgender high school student to use the restroom corresponding to his gender identity.[2] In 2015, a county clerk in Kentucky refused to issue marriage licenses to same-sex couples.[3] All claimed that sincerely held Christian beliefs exempted them from treating certain folks as neighbors. Really?

Since the beginning of the coronavirus pandemic, members of the Religious Right across the United States have stubbornly refused to follow social distancing guidelines, wear masks in public, or get vaccinated. These people who have recklessly endangered the lives and health of their neighbors have often claimed that their refusal to comply with proven public health guidelines is based on sincerely held Christian beliefs.[4]

Yet what exactly are the beliefs to which these people appeal? For those who identify as Christians, do those as-yet-unspecified beliefs truly outweigh the preeminence that Jesus conferred upon the biblical injunction to love one's neighbor?

---

1   Adam Liptak, "Justices to Hear Case on Religious Objections to Same-Sex Marriage," 26 June 2017, nytimes.com.
2   Matt Stevens, "Transgender Student in Bathroom Dispute Wins Court Ruling," 22 May 2018, nytimes.com.
3   Alan Blinder and Richard Pérez-Peña, "County Clerk Denies Same-Sex Marriage Licenses, Defying Court," 1 September 2015, nytimes.com.
4   Ruth Graham, "Vaccine Resisters Seek Religious Exemptions. But What Counts as Religious?" 11 September 2021, nytimes.com.

MEDITATION 8

"[S]hould I not be concerned about Nineveh, that great city,
in which there are more than a hundred and twenty thousand persons
who do not know their right hand from their left,
and also many animals?"

—JONAH 4:11

ONCE THE DEITY HAS DIRECTED THIS POINTED QUESTION TO JONAH, the story abruptly ends, without revealing the prophet's response. Thus, readers themselves must supply an answer, which discloses the author's design. The obligation imposed on readers to provide the story's resolution supplies the final clue (if earlier hints have gone unnoticed) that this story was never meant to be read as a straightforward historical narrative.

Most churchgoers recall the story's opening act, the part that they learned in Sunday school. The deity calls Jonah to proclaim judgment upon Nineveh because of its people's wickedness, but the prophet disobeys, booking passage on a ship bound in the opposite direction. During a storm at sea, the crew throws him overboard and a huge fish swallows him. Then, after Jonah has spent three days in the belly of the fish, his divine call is renewed.

Given a second chance, Jonah warns the people of Nineveh of their impending doom, but what happens next leaves some readers a bit disoriented. According to the story, the entire city heeds the prophet's message and repents in sackcloth and ashes, whereupon the deity relents and averts his judgment. Jonah, incensed by this turn of events, admits in a devastated lament that such an outcome had been his worst fear all along.

The last scene involves a simple object lesson drawn from nature, one that sets the stage for the deity's crucial inquiry.

Jonah voices his furious indignation over the demise of a large bush that had briefly shaded him from the elements. In response, the deity asks the prophet to compare his own concern for an ephemeral plant with the deity's concern for the hitherto clueless people of Nineveh and their livestock.

As this story's original audience understood quite well, none of what it describes reflects factual events. The story of Jonah is a parable. As such, it is designed to make people think—in this instance, to think about whether the deity's proper concern extends to his chosen people alone or to pagans as well. The deity's unanswered query invites a reconsideration of the entrenched prejudices of a nationalist mind-set.

The Religious Right has invariably conflated its vision of national destiny with the will of the biblical deity. The world heard that sentiment expressed in President George W. Bush's speech at the National Cathedral after the terrorist attacks of September 11, 2001: "But our responsibility to history is already clear: to answer these attacks and rid the world of evil."[1] Without hesitation, he presumed that this nation and the causes that it pursues are necessarily good.

When Bush later led the nation to war under false pretenses, military leaders (including the commander-in-chief) showed no interest in Iraqi body counts, combatant or civilian.[2] Evidently, Bush's "compassionate conservatism"[3] did not apply beyond America's borders. One imagines the biblical deity saying to Bush and his supporters on the Religious Right, "Listen, your brother's blood is crying out to me from the ground!" (Gen 4:9).

---

1 "Remarks by the President: President George W. Bush," 14 September 2001, cathedral.org.
2 John M. Broder, "A Nation at War: The Casualties; U.S. Military Has No Account of Iraqi Dead in Fighting," 2 April 2003, nytimes.com.
3 Alison Mitchell, "Bush Draws Campaign Theme from More Than 'the Heart,'" 12 June 2000, nytimes.com.

MEDITATION 9

For the time is coming when people will not put up with sound doctrine,
but having itching ears, they will accumulate for themselves
teachers to suit their own desires,
and will turn away from listening to the
truth and wander away to myths.

—2 TIMOTHY 4:3–4

TRADITION DESIGNATES THE THREE LETTERS ADDRESSED TO PAUL'S
protégés Timothy and Titus as the Pastoral Letters because
they focus on the offices of pastoral leadership and over-
sight within the church. Their significant differences from
the apostle's undisputed letters have led most critical scholars to infer that they are pseudonymous, composed by an
unknown writer who used Paul's authority to offer ecclesi-
astical guidance to a subsequent generation.

Christians who reject the methods of historical critical
research still accept the authenticity of the Pastorals. However, unless they limit the application of the present text to
its first century context and deny it any meaningful relevance
for twenty-first century believers, the question of Pauline au-
thorship does not undermine the analysis that follows. Indeed, the discussion below retains the conventional names
of the letter's author and addressee.

As a good mentor, Paul prepares Timothy for the future,
a time when his young coworker will no longer have the
benefit of the apostle's direct counsel. He warns his protégé
that not all converts to the gospel will remain faithful to
its message. He alerts him to the likelihood that some people who "confess with [their] lips that Jesus is Lord" (Rom
10:9) will, nonetheless, forsake their calling and abandon
his teaching.

Unfortunately, historians lack sufficient evidence to identify the type of false teaching that prompted Paul's concern. Various biblical commentaries offer a range of speculation but little consensus. Subsequent church history, of course, offers many examples of the kind of apostasy that the apostle anticipated. Indeed, the ways that Christians have strayed from "the faith that was once for all entrusted to the saints" (Jude 1:3) are legion.

Today is no different. Despite its stated goal of restoring Christian values to the public square, the Religious Right has had little constructive impact on American politics. Instead, as theologian Catherine Keller observes, politics has exerted a far greater influence in the other direction. She coins the term "Foxangelicals" to describe Christians whose perspective owes more to the punditry of Fox News than it does to the precepts of the Bible.[1]

According to John Compton, evidence confirms that observation: "Seemingly every day, a new poll finds white evangelicals—by far the largest subset of American Protestants—espousing views that would appear difficult to reconcile with the golden rule." As his research demonstrates, white evangelicals deny the economic effects of systemic racism, favor sharp reductions in legal immigration, and support funding cuts for social welfare programs.[2]

The Religious Right spurns what the Bible teaches about caring for the poor, the hungry, the sick, and the alien (Zech 7:10; Mt 25:35–36). Instead, its members tune in to pundits, rally around politicians, and flock to preachers who tell them only what they want to hear.

---

1   Catherine Keller, "Foxangelicals, Political Theology, and Friends," in *Doing Theology in the Age of Trump*, ed. Jeffrey W. Robbins and Clayton Crockett (Eugene, OR: Cascade Books, 2018), 94.
2   John W. Compton, *The End of Empathy: Why White Protestants Stopped Loving Their Neighbors* (New York: Oxford University Press, 2020), 1.

MEDITATION 10

What has been is what will be,
and what has been done is what will be done;
there is nothing new under the sun.

—ECCLESIASTES 1:9

ECCLESIASTES, AN UNCONVENTIONAL EXAMPLE OF HEBREW WISDOM literature, concerns itself with general reflections about the meaning of life. Tradition attributes the book to Solomon because its author identifies himself as "the Teacher, the son of David" (1:1) and describes his life at the royal court in extravagant terms (2:1–12). Linguistic clues, though, have led critical scholars to date the work to the fourth century BCE, long after Solomon's lifetime.

The assertion that "there is nothing new under the sun" is a proverb, a well-known general truth based on practical experience. As such, it reflects an expression of human perception, not divine revelation. Should readers treat this statement as a superficial remark or as a provocative insight, one that invites further reflection? The answer to that question depends on the context in which it is found, on the seriousness of the subject at hand.

Consider a topic mentioned elsewhere in these pages: the voter-suppression measures enacted by red-state legislatures across the nation, laws that have had a disproportionate impact on voters of color. Because they disenfranchise Black voters in the same way that Jim Crow laws once did, some have dubbed them "Jim Crow 2.0."[1] Their passage exemplifies all too well the warning that "what has been done is what will be done."

1 Charles M. Blow, "Welcome to Jim Crow 2.0," 14 July 2021, nytimes.com.

Consider the furor that erupted when President Joe Biden drew several pointed analogies to challenge members of the Senate to end their filibuster and take up voting rights legislation. "Do you want to be on the side of Dr. King or George Wallace?" he asked. "Do you want to be on the side of John Lewis or Bull Connor?" In response to the histrionic outrage that ensued, Professor Eddie Glaude aptly deemed the Republican reaction "disingenuous."[2]

After signing the Civil Rights Act of 1964, President Lyndon Johnson told press aide Bill Moyers, "I think we just delivered the South to the Republican Party for a long time to come."[3] History proved him correct. Richard Nixon developed his "Southern strategy" to increase political support among disaffected white voters and allow the Republican Party to replace the Democratic Party as "the vehicle of white supremacy in the South."[4]

No one should be surprised that racists shifted their party allegiance. The ideology of white supremacy has always found a haven in American politics: "there is nothing new under the sun." What is surprising—or, at least, should be— is that so many white Christians in America have consistently aligned themselves with the party most amenable to white supremacy. If "what has been is what will be," then "America's original sin"[5] may yet prove fatal.

---

2   Ashley Parker, "Biden Defends His Bull Connor Analogy after Republicans Charge Him with Crossing a Line," 21 January 2022, washingtonpost.com.
3   Michael Oreskes, "Civil Rights Act Leaves Deep Mark on the American Political Landscape," 2 July 1989, nytimes.com.
4   R. W. Apple, Jr., "GOP Tries Hard to Win Black Votes, but Recent History Works Against It," 19 September 1996, nytimes.com.
5   Jim Wallis, *America's Original Sin: Racism, White Privilege, and a Bridge to a New America*, (Grand Rapids: Brazos, 2016.

MEDITATION 11

But the midwives feared God;
they did not do as the king of Egypt commanded them,
but they let the boys live.

—EXODUS 1:17

THE OPENING SCENES IN EXODUS SKETCH IN BROAD STROKES THE cruel oppression suffered by the Israelites during their sojourn in Egypt, including their subjection to forced labor and Pharaoh's attempt to check their proliferation by ordering the midwives to kill all male infants at birth. The disclosure of the midwives' names, Shiphrah and Puah, in contrast to the anonymity of the reigning Pharoah alerts readers to the narrator's primary interest.

Modern readers sometimes misconstrue what it means when the narrator says that "the midwives feared God." Here, the word *fear* denotes not an emotion of terror or dread but an action commensurate with the deity's moral authority. The midwives have every reason to cower before the Egyptian Pharaoh because he is undoubtedly the most powerful man on earth. To disregard his direct command is to risk death. Nonetheless, they brazenly defy him.

Prior to the Civil War, abolitionists not only pursued political efforts to end slavery in the United States but also deliberately violated existing laws by providing safe houses along the route of the Underground Railroad to help enslaved people escape into free states and Canada. Not all abolitionists were Christians, but those who were defied the law as an act of faith. Like their counterparts in Exodus, they acknowledged a higher moral authority.

In 2018, the Trump administration put into effect its infamous family separation policy, a measure under which federal authorities separated migrant children and infants from parents or guardians who had entered the United States without proper authorization—including political refugees fleeing violence in their home countries. Incredibly, this unprecedented policy included no provisions or funding for reuniting family members later.[1]

The public outcry was swift and resolute, including strong denunciations from prominent religious leaders. Cardinal Daniel DiNardo, president of the U.S. Conference of Catholic Bishops, called the policy "immoral," and Rabbi Jonah Dov Pesner, director of the Religious Action Center, called it "unconscionable."[2]

Still, one faith community failed to join the chorus against Trump's policy. Despite biblical mandates to welcome strangers and not deprive them of justice (Deut 24:17; Jer 22:3; Mt 25:43), white Evangelicals were reluctant to criticize their anointed leader.[3] Robert Jeffress, pastor of First Baptist Church in Dallas, spoke for many fellow evangelicals when he glibly asserted, "There's nothing un-Christian about government protecting its borders."[4]

Throughout history, some Christians have defied the ruling authorities rather than comply with inhumane policies. Nowadays, inexplicably, many white evangelicals and white Catholics endorse such policies.

1 Maya Rhodan, "Here Are the Facts about Trump's Family Separation Policy," 20 June 2018, time.com. Southern Poverty Law Center, "Family Separation under the Trump Administration—a Timeline," 17 June 2020, splcenter.org.

2 Sasha Ingber, "Faith Leaders Oppose Trump's Immigration Policy of Separating Children from Parents," 16 June 2018, npr.org.

3 Michelle Boorstein and Julie Zauzmer, "Many White Evangelicals Are Not Protesting Family Separations on the U.S. Border," 18 June 2018, washingtonpost.com.

4 Sarah Posner, *Unholy: Why White Evangelicals Worship at the Altar of Donald Trump* (New York: Random House, 2020), 38.

MEDITATION 12

Happy are those who do not follow the advice of the wicked,
or take the path that sinners tread, or sit in the seat of scoffers;
but their delight is in the law of the LORD,
and on his law they meditate day and night.

—PSALM 1:1–2

THESE OPENING LINES PROVIDE A FITTING INTRODUCTION TO THE
entire Psalter by contrasting two disparate ways of life.
The psalmist initially characterizes the more excellent way
through a series of negations, each of which clarifies something that good people instinctively avoid: the counsel that
they rebuff, the course that they reject, and the company
that they shun. The moral choices that they make prevent
them from being drawn into destructive pursuits.

Good people, the psalmist says, avoid such misguided
inclinations by focusing their attention on "the law of the
LORD." Because the rather narrow connotations of the English word *law* fail to convey the scope of what the Hebrew
word *torah* denotes, a paraphrase seems helpful: The way of
life that the psalmist commends is one in which people find
their direction and purpose not in the commandments alone,
but in all that the Scriptures teach.

In principle, the church has traditionally adopted this
same approach. The Christian way of life is one grounded in
the teachings of Scripture, teachings embodied in the life and
work of Jesus. In practice, however, far too many churchgoers have failed to pursue that way of life consistently. As the
English writer G. K. Chesterton once quipped, "The Christian ideal has not been tried and found wanting. It has been
found difficult; and left untried."[1]

Many members of the Religious Right no longer let the Bible shape their political views; another source has usurped its place. Jonathan Martin, himself an evangelical pastor, has observed the problem first-hand: "A pastor has about 30 to 40 minutes each week to teach [parishioners] about Scripture," he says. "They've been exposed to Fox News potentially three to four hours a day." "Now," he contends, "the Bible's increasingly irrelevant. It's just 'us versus them.'"[2]

Recall President Trump's Muslim Ban. In response to that executive order, 100 prominent evangelical leaders published a full-page ad in *The Washington Post* denouncing the policy because it directly contradicted biblical teaching.[3] Nonetheless, a Pew Research survey found that three-quarters (76%) of white evangelicals approved of the ban.[4] They clearly had little interest in what the Bible had to say about the matter.

Not long after evangelist Jerry Falwell founded the Moral Majority in 1979, critics began attacking its positions by declaring, "The Moral Majority is neither."[5] If Jonathan Martin is correct when he suggests that the teaching of Scripture has become "increasingly irrelevant" to many members of the Religious Right, then what exactly does the term *religious* signify in the ongoing conflict that pits "us versus them"?

---

1   G. K. Chesterton, "The Unfinished Temple," in *What's Wrong with the World* (New York: Sheed and Ward, 1956), 27.

2   Amy Sullivan, "America's New Religion: Fox Evangelicalism," 15 December 2017, nytimes.com.

3   Sarah Pulliam Bailey, "Conservative Evangelicals Join Letter Denouncing Trump's Order on Refugees," 8 February 2017, washingtonpost.com. Press Release, "Evangelical Leaders from All 50 States Urge President Trump to Reconsider Reduction in Refugee Resettlement," 8 February 2017, worldrelief.org.

4   Gregory A. Smith, "Most White Evangelicals Approve of Trump Travel Prohibition and Express Concerns about Extremism," 27 February 2017, pewresearch.org.

5   Carl Golden, Jr., "A Look at the Moral Majority," 24 January 1982, nytimes.com.

MEDITATION 13

In the same way, let your light shine before others,
so that they may see your good works
and give glory to your Father in heaven.
—Matthew 5:16

To understand any statement, one must consider its context. That is certainly the case here because this statement's initial phrase points readers back to preceding assertions. The context in this instance is the Sermon on the Mount, a discourse by Jesus addressed to people who embrace his teaching. According to Jesus, his followers play an indispensable role in a society where most folks have adopted a different way of life.

Jesus describes that vital role in figurative terms: "You are the light of the world" (5:14a). By characterizing his followers' purpose in terms of light's relationship to darkness, he is telling them that they will inevitably be conspicuous: "A city set on a hill cannot be hid" (5:14b). Part of what that suggests is that, for good or for ill, people who identify themselves as followers of Jesus ultimately have no place to hide.

Alert readers realize that, in most circumstances, a light's function is not to be seen but to make it easier for people to see other things. Thus, Jesus is telling his followers that if they accept their role, if they fulfill their calling, their actions will make it easier for other people to discern the deity's presence more clearly. Of course, if they betray their calling, other people will observe that as well.

In 2016, Donald Trump campaigned on the slogan "Make America Great Again." Based on what he said at his rallies and which applause lines drew the loudest response, what he and his supporters had in mind was an idealized vision of a white Christian America before the civil rights legislation of the 1960s ended Jim Crow[1] and before comparable reforms lifted discriminatory restrictions against immigrants from Asia, Africa, the Middle East and Eastern Europe.[2]

On election day that year, 81% of white Evangelicals and 60% of white Catholics voted for Trump.[3] In doing so, those Christians revealed the content of their faith. Jesus called them to love their neighbors, to welcome strangers, and to help those in need (Mt 22:39; Mt 25:35–36), but they voted for a man who pledged to roll back civil rights protections, to enact exclusionary policies toward immigrants, and to make funding cuts in social programs.

Those Christians left no doubt about whom they serve. They left no doubt about whom they hope gets all the glory.

---

1 The Civil Rights Act of 1964 and the Voting Rights Act of 1965.
2 The Immigration and Nationality Act of 1965.
3 Jessica Martínez and Gregory A. Smith, "How the Faithful Voted: A Preliminary 2016 Analysis," 9 November 2016, pewresearch.org.

MEDITATION 14

[Jesus said,] "The scribes and the Pharisees sit on Moses' seat;
therefore, do whatever they teach you and follow it;
but do not do as they do, for they do not practice what they teach."
—Matthew 23:2–3

There is a big difference, Jesus says, between what people say and what they do. The scribes and Pharisees share the teaching of Scripture with a populace that is largely illiterate, so Jesus' listeners can ill afford to ignore their words. Nonetheless, Jesus warns against following those leaders' example because their hypocrisy betrays the content of their character.

Recall the political firestorm that erupted in 1998 following the revelation of Bill Clinton's sexual dalliance with a 24-year-old White House intern. Clinton initially denied the allegations of misconduct, but eventually the intern's testimony about their relationship and the evidence of her semen-stained dress forced him to acknowledge the truth.

James Dobson, founder of Focus on the Family, proved Clinton's most vocal critic. In a 1998 newsletter to supporters, he described Clinton's "disregard for morality" as "profoundly disturbing." Dobson blamed "the mainstream media" for downplaying Clinton's indiscretions with the excuse that "character doesn't matter." He rebuked various members of the press by name for their efforts "to undermine the moral values that we call 'character.'"

Insisting that "character DOES matter," Dobson rejected the popular notion that Clinton's personal misconduct had no bearing on his capacity to lead the nation. He concluded his jeremiad with a dire warning: "[O]ur greatest problem is not in the Oval Office. It is with the people of this land! We have lost our ability to discern the difference between right and wrong.... And when a nation reaches that state of depravity—judgment is a certainty."[1]

Fast-forward to the 2016 presidential campaign when *The Washington Post* broke its story about the *Access Hollywood* tape on which Donald Trump bragged about assaulting women.[2] The Religious Right had already thrown its support behind the thrice-married adulterer and admitted sexual predator,[3] and little had been said about the character issue. However, the tape's release, one month before the election, brought out the heavy hitters.

Jerry Falwell, Jr., president of Liberty University, dismissed Trump's words as "dumb comments on a videotape 11 years ago." Ralph Reed, chairman of the Faith and Freedom Coalition, and Tony Perkins, president of the Family Research Council, doubled down on their endorsement of Trump. Even James Dobson voiced continued support for Trump.[4] As writer Sarah Posner observed, "The era of the 'values voter' was over."[5]

To paraphrase Dobson's 1998 lament: Members of the Religious Right have lost their ability to care about the difference between right and wrong.

---

1 James Dobson, Online Newsletter, September 1998, http://ontology. buffalo.edu/smith/clinton/character.html, (emphasis original).

2 David A. Fahrenthold, "Trump Recorded Having Extremely Lewd Conversation about Women in 2005," 8 October 2016, washingtonpost. com.

3 Tierney McAfee, "A New Wife, Baby, and Two Alleged Mistresses: Inside Donald Trump's World in 2006," 7 March 2018, people.com.

4 Eugene Scott, Ashley Killough, and Daniel Burke, "Evangelicals 'Disgusted' by Trump's Remarks, But Still Backing Him," 21 October 2016, cnn.com.

5 Sarah Posner, *Unholy: Why White Evangelicals Worship at the Altar of Donald Trump* (New York: Random House, 2020), xviii.

MEDITATION 15

[Jesus] said to him,
"What is written in the law?
What do you read there?"

—LUKE 10:26

A LAWYER—AN EXPERT IN THE PRECEPTS OF THE TORAH—ASKS Jesus a question: "Teacher, what must I do to inherit eternal life?" (10:25). Jesus, aware that this request for information is likely a test, responds with the two queries here. So the man answers his own question, reciting the sacred words of the Torah from memory: One must give one's ultimate devotion to the deity alone (Deut 6:5), and one must regard one's neighbor as oneself (Lev 19:18).

Jesus commends the lawyer, telling him, "You have given the right answer; do this, and you will live" (10:28). The exchange does not end there, though, because the lawyer poses a new question: "And who is my neighbor?" (10:29). Focusing on the second biblical mandate, he says, in effect, "I have told you what is written in the law; now you tell me what you read there." In other words, "What exactly does the word *neighbor* mean in this context?"

By asking the question, "And who is my neighbor?" the lawyer has unwittingly revealed how he himself reads Scripture. He seemingly takes for granted that there must be certain exceptions. He reads the Torah in a way that limits his responsibility toward others. However, as churchgoers recall, Jesus answers the lawyer's second question with the parable of the good Samaritan, a story suggesting that there are no exceptions.

29

Consider the following comments by Jerry Falwell, Jr., in a *Washington Post* interview. "It's such a distortion of the teachings of Jesus," he insisted, "to say that what he taught us to do personally—to love our neighbors as ourselves, help the poor—can somehow be imputed on [sic] a nation. Jesus never told Caesar how to run Rome." Falwell flatly rejected the idea that "public policy should be dictated by the teachings of Jesus."[1]

Falwell and other like-minded Christians fail to see the irony of that position. When it came to securing tax-exempt status for their segregation academies, they had no qualms about telling Caesar how to run Washington. Today, when it comes to their own narrow-minded views about abortion, same-sex marriage, or turning away Muslim immigrants, they do try to dictate public policy. They just do so in ways diametrically opposed to the teachings of Jesus.

In that *Post* interview, Falwell spoke volumes. He revealed everything that people need to know about how members of the Religious Right choose to read the Bible. They assume that they can compartmentalize life by separating what they view as personal religious decisions from what they view as corporate civic duties. Like the lawyer in Luke's story, they are looking for loopholes, some way to avoid the moral ramifications of their professed faith.

There is a reason that Jesus deliberately distinguishes two separate issues. The second part of what he asks the lawyer may be one of the most profound questions ever raised. When Jesus asks, "What do you read there?" he is pressing the lawyer to do more than simply quote the words of Scripture. He is forcing him to explain what those words mean—to confront their ethical demands, to accept their practical, costly implications.

---

1   Joe Heim, "Jerry Falwell Jr. Can't Imagine Trump 'Doing Anything That's Not Good for the Country,'" 1 January 2019, washingtonpost.com.

MEDITATION 16

Jesus said to them,
"Give to the emperor the things that are the emperor's
and to God the things that are God's."

—MARK 12:17

JESUS' ADVERSARIES HOPE "TO TRAP HIM IN WHAT HE SAID," SO they pose a duplicitous question: "Is it lawful to pay taxes to the emperor or not?" (12:13–14). It appears that, no matter what Jesus says, his words will be used against him. If he says, "Yes, it is lawful," he will lose popular support from those who begrudge subsidizing the pagan army that occupies their homeland; yet, if he says, "No, it is not lawful," he will be subject to immediate arrest.

So, Jesus refuses to provide a straight yes-or-no response. Instead, he asks to see a denarius, the Roman coin used to pay the tax. With that coin in hand, Jesus poses his own question, "Whose head is this, and whose title?" and his adversaries reply, "The emperor's" (12:16). Jesus then ends the discussion with the enigmatic statement here—one that requires serious consideration from everyone who encounters it, not just his original audience.

The popular understanding of Jesus' words suggests that folks can neatly compartmentalize life. According to that view, "the things that are the emperor's" would include the secular realm of politics and government, while "the things that are God's" would be limited to the religious realm of individual beliefs and personal morality. That interpretation, though, totally distorts what Jesus has said. It cedes far too much authority to the state.

31

Robert Jeffress, the pastor of First Baptist Church in Dallas, resorted to this specious interpretation to maintain that the teaching of Jesus has no relevance for American immigration policy. Referring to Central American refugee children seeking asylum at the nation's southern border, Jeffress said, "Yes, Jesus loved children, but he also respected law. He said, render unto Caesar the things that are Caesars [sic]."[1]

Jerry Falwell, Jr., the president of Liberty University, used the same misguided approach to justify every policy implemented during Donald Trump's first two years in office. He said, "[Jesus] went out of his way to say that's the earthly kingdom, I'm about the heavenly kingdom and I'm here to teach you how to treat others, how to help others, but when it comes to serving your country, you render unto Caesar that which is Caesar's."[2]

Jeffress, Falwell, and others like them have misconstrued these words because they assume that both parts of Jesus' statement have equal significance, but that is not the case. By introducing the idea of one's ultimate obligation to the deity, Jesus relativizes one's obligation to the state. Indeed, one's obligation to the deity encompasses every aspect of human existence, public as well as private, political as well as religious.

To condone official injustice is to betray the Christian faith. One of Jesus' earliest followers put it this way: "We must obey God rather than any human authority" (Acts 5:29).

---

1   Alan Bean, "Dallas Preacher Says Jesus Would Seal the Border," 15 July 2014, baptistnews.com.
2   Joe Heim, "Jerry Falwell Jr. Can't Imagine Trump 'Doing Anything That's Not Good for the Country,'" 1 January 2019, washingtonpost.com.

MEDITATION 17

"Should I mourn and practice abstinence in the fifth month,
as I have done for so many years?"

—Zechariah 7:3

This text is likely unfamiliar to most churchgoers. However, the story in which it appears remains relevant to believers of every generation. Devout people from Bethel send a delegation to ask the religious authorities in Jerusalem a question about proper religious practice. For years they have observed a time of penitence and fasting to commemorate the destruction of the Temple by the Babylonians in 586 BCE (2 Kings 25:9).

These folks want to know whether to continue that time-honored tradition. After all, a remnant of the Jewish people has returned from exile in Babylon, just as the former prophets had promised, and now the Temple itself is being rebuilt. So, should they continue to dwell on what happened in the past, or has the time come to focus on the future? It is a legitimate question: Is the ritual still relevant?

The prophet responds with a question of his own: "When you fasted in the fifth month...for these seventy years, was it for [the Lord] that you fasted?" (7:5). A question about personal piety has become an issue of individual integrity. Zechariah then points the petitioners to some of the most powerful pronouncements of the prophetic tradition: "Render true judgments...do not oppress the widow, the orphan, the alien, or the poor" (7:9–10).

The prophets of old never talked about when to fast; that was never an issue. On the other hand, they repeatedly

33

urged people to provide for the poor and to protect the powerless. According to Scripture, those concerns have always taken precedence over the practice of piety. Devotion to the deity is not about whether devout people fast on a holy day; it is about whether needy people have enough to eat on all the other days.

Recall the uproar over the so-called "War on Christmas" that has become a major issue for the Religious Right in recent years. Fox News host Bill O'Reilly told viewers that replacing the greeting, "Merry Christmas," with the more inclusive greeting, "Happy Holidays," amounted to an attack on Christian beliefs. Donald Trump even campaigned on the issue, promising supporters that he would put an end to such secular assaults.[1]

The celebration of Christmas was never under attack, but Trump's election did affect people's celebration of the holiday. His administration approved a rule change that would deny 700,000 Americans access to food stamps, a move bitterly denounced by Senator Chuck Schumer of New York: "The Trump administration is driving the vulnerable into hunger just as the Christmas season approaches."[2]

If members of the Religious Right get more upset over folks saying "Happy Holidays" than they do over the government cutting food stamps for hundreds of thousands of low-income families, then they are neglecting what Jesus called "the weightier matters of the law: justice and mercy and faith" (Mt 23:23).

---

1 Liam Stack, "How the 'War on Christmas' Controversy Was Created," 19 December 2016, nytimes.com.
2 Lola Fadulu, "Hundreds of Thousands Are Losing Access to Food Stamps," 2 December 2019, nytimes.com.

MEDITATION 18

Ah, you who call evil good and good evil....

—Isaiah 5:20

Isaiah's complaint begins with the word *Ah*, an interjection used to express his disgust with the sophistry of people whose attitudes and actions prove that they have no moral compass. As his scathing indictment makes clear, their inability to distinguish right and wrong has a dual cause: they "are wise in [their] own eyes" (5:21) and "have rejected the instruction of the LORD of hosts" (5:24). The resulting social injustice will not go unpunished (5:23–24).

On August 12, 2017, various white supremacist groups assembled in Charlottesville, Virginia, for the "Unite the Right" rally, a public protest ostensibly occasioned by the decision to remove a statue of Robert E. Lee from a city park. These white nationalists, neo-Nazis, and members of the Ku Klux Klan chanted racist and anti-Semitic slogans. Many carried Confederate flags or placards with fascist symbols.[1]

A group made up of local clergy, racial justice activists, and concerned residents staged a counterprotest to voice their opposition to these white supremacists. Unfortunately, members of antifa who joined the counterprotest refused to honor its commitment to nonviolence.[2] When fighting erupt-

---

1 Joe Heim, Ellie Silverman, T. Rees Shapiro, and Emma Brown, "One Dead as Car Strikes Crowds Amid Protests of White Nationalist Gathering in Charlottesville; Two Police Die in Helicopter Crash," 13 August 2017, washingtonpost.com
2 Farah Stockman, "Who Were the Counterprotesters in Charlottesville?" 14 August 2017, nytimes.com.

ed between the rival groups, the governor declared a state of emergency and police in riot gear cleared the scene.[3]

That same day, Donald Trump held a news conference in Bedminster, New Jersy, during which he addressed events in Charlottesville. He said, "We condemn in the strongest possible terms this egregious display of hatred, bigotry and violence on many sides, on many sides."[4] Critics immediately faulted Trump for insinuating a moral equivalence between the various white supremacist groups and those who opposed them.

Republican Senator Cory Gardner of Colorado was among the critics, writing on Twitter: "Mr. President—we must call evil by its name. These were white supremacists, and this was domestic terrorism."[5]

On August 15, Trump held a news conference in New York City during which he again addressed the controversial events. After blaming both sides for the violence, a point that no one disputes, he said, "But you also had people that were very fine people on both sides."[6] Despite the reaction to his earlier remarks, he refused to draw any meaningful distinction between advocates of white supremacy and people who oppose that ideology.

In describing white supremacists as "very fine people," Trump called evil good. In giving this unprincipled individual their continued support, members of the Religious Right have done the same thing.

---

3 Sheryl Gay Stolberg, "Hurt and Angry, Charlottesville Tries to Regroup from Violence," 13 August 2017.
4 Carly Sitrin, "Read: President Trump's Remarks Condemning Violence 'on Many Sides' in Charlottesville," 12 August 2017, vox.com.
5 Glenn Thrush and Maggie Haberman, "Trump Is Criticized for Not Calling Out White Supremacists," 13 August 2017, nytimes.com.
6 The New York Times, "Full Transcript and Video: Trump's News Conference in New York," 15 August 2017, nytimes.com

MEDITATION 19

Then they also will answer,
"Lord, when was it that we saw you hungry or thirsty
or a stranger or naked or sick or in prison,
and did not take care of you?"
Then he will answer them, "Truly I tell you, just as you did not do it
to one of the least of these, you did not do it to me."
—MATTHEW 25:44–45

MOST CHURCHGOERS KNOW THE STORY IN WHICH THESE WORDS appear as the parable of the sheep and the goats. Jesus uses the story to clarify the standard by which all people will ultimately be judged. According to the story, the final judgment has nothing to do with whether an individual has made a profession of faith. The only thing that matters, Jesus says, is whether someone has acted with compassion toward people in need.

Some churches have a food pantry or run a soup kitchen that helps to address the problem of hunger in their communities, and many other churches support such efforts. Unfortunately, those measures cannot do nearly enough. With thirty-eight million people living in food-insecure households,[1] the United States must rely on government programs to provide services that private organizations alone almost certainly could not sustain.[2]

Nevertheless, in 2017, Donald Trump and congressional Republicans proposed a budget that included major tax breaks for corporations and wealthy individuals that were

---

1 Feedingamerica.org/hunger-in-america.
2 Emma Green, "Can Religious Charities Take the Place of the Welfare State?" 26 March 2017, theatlantic.com.

37

paid for by drastic cuts to various social programs designed to help low-income Americans, including the Supplemental Nutrition Assistance Program (food stamps), Medicaid, and Temporary Assistance for Needy Families (welfare).[3]

As religion professor Julie Ingersoll observed at the time, those proposed budget cuts were consistent with political views held by members of the Religious Right. For several decades, they have maintained that "the role of civil government is limited to the protection of property and the punishment of criminals."[4] According to author and educator Heather McGhee, the emergence of that antigovernment sentiment coincided with the rise of white grievance.[5]

In the story that Jesus tells, he makes no mention of extenuating circumstances. Unlike members of the Religious Right, his concern is indiscriminate. He sees the divine image in every human being in need, irrespective of that person's skin color, ethnicity, or sexual orientation. Jesus talks about feeding the hungry and welcoming strangers, and he expects his followers to act accordingly, regardless of whether those people seem deserving.

When members of the Religious Right see someone in need, their main concern seems to be whether that person is trying to game the system and get something for nothing. What they fail to see, when they encounter someone in need, is the face of Jesus.

---

3 Yamiche Alcindor, "Trump Budget Cuts Programs for Poor While Sparing Many Older People," 22 May 2017, nytimes.com.
4 Julie Ingersoll, "Why Trump's Evangelicals Won't Care about Those Budget Cuts," 25 May 2017, religiondispatches.org.
5 Heather McGhee, *The Sum of Us: What Racism Costs Everyone and How We Can Prosper Together* (New York: One World, 2021), 28–39.

MEDITATION 20

Elijah then came near to all the people, and said,
"How long will you go limping with two different opinions?
If the LORD is God, follow him; but if Baal, then follow him."
The people did not answer him a word.

—1 KINGS 18:21

THE TRANSLATION "LIMPING" MUDDLES THE HEBREW METAPHOR, which suggests a bird flitting back and forth between two branches. Thus, Elijah's rhetorical question depicts the Israelite people in unflattering terms, suggesting that they cannot make up their minds. Yet the time has come for them to choose. Either serve Baal, the Canaanite storm deity, or serve the deity that they know as Yahweh (Ex 6:3), the maker of heaven and earth.

For the ancient Israelites, the choice between these two religions had practical economic implications. They wanted to remain true to Yahweh, but they had seen many of their Canaanite neighbors reap a bountiful harvest after offering sacrifices to Baal. So, the Israelites convinced themselves that they could hedge their bets by offering sacrifices to both deities. However, according to Elijah, that was not an option.

Today, members of the Religious Right face a similar quandary. For more than seven years now, they have been flitting back and forth between two antithetical positions. On the one hand, they proudly call themselves Christians and confidently claim that Jesus Christ is Lord of their lives; on the other hand, their obsequious devotion to Donald Trump quite often determines what they think, what they say, and what they do.

According to Scripture, such duplicity fools no one: "Whoever says, 'I have come to know [Christ],' but does not obey his commandments, is a liar, and in such a person the truth does not exist" (1 Jn 2:4). Jesus specifically warned against such hypocrisy: "Not everyone who says to me, 'Lord, Lord,' will enter the kingdom of heaven, but only the one who does the will of my father in heaven" (Mt 7:21).

Members of the Religious Right need to spend more time reading their Bibles. They need to rediscover what the Scriptures have to say about caring for the people that society counts least and puts last. They should admit that there is nothing recognizably Christian in Trump's vindictive pronouncements and divisive politics. The time has come to choose. If Jesus is Lord, then follow him. If not, then keep following Trump.

MEDITATION 21

If our God whom we serve is able to deliver us
from the furnace of blazing fire and out of your hand,
O king, let him deliver us.
But if not, be it known to you, O king,
that we will not serve your gods
and we will not worship the golden statue that you have set up.
—Daniel 3:17–18

Taken at face value, the accounts in the Book of Daniel report events that took place in the sixth century BCE; however, various clues scattered throughout the book confirm that these tales represent not straightforward historical narratives but religious folklore. Thus, the value of these stories, like the parables of Jesus, lies not in the historical accuracy of what they describe but in the theological message that they impart.

In the present scene, three Israelite exiles have refused to comply with the Babylonian king's decree that everyone bow down to the idolatrous image that he has erected. Aware that their disobedience is quite literally a matter of life and death, they remain defiant. With no assurance that divine deliverance is forthcoming, they have resolved to do the right thing, regardless of the consequences. For them, martyrdom is preferable to apostasy.

In 1944, the Gestapo arrested Casper ten Boom for harboring Jewish refugees in his home. The authorities offered to release him if he promised to discontinue such efforts. "If I go home today," he said, "tomorrow I will open my door again to any man in need who knocks."[1] With his life in the balance,

---

1 Corrie ten Boom with John and Elizabeth Sherrill, *The Hiding Place: The Triumphant Story of Corrie ten Boom* (New York: Bantam Books, 1974), 137–138.

the old Dutchman left no doubt about what he would do.

Since Donald Trump's political ascendancy within the Republican Party, most leaders of the Religious Right have failed to speak truth to power. Indeed, as columnist Michael Gerson observes, they have usually played the role of "sycophants," with their rush "to provide Trump political cover in every scandal and offer preemptive absolution of every character failure."[2] Where are today's exemplars of faith like the ones depicted in Daniel?

Rest assured, such people do exist, and they have spoken out clearly and forcefully. During the 2016 presidential campaign, more than 22,000 people signed "A Declaration by American Evangelicals Concerning Donald Trump," a public statement posted by evangelical leaders on change.org. Those leaders, representing a wide range of Christian churches and denominations, left no doubt about where they stood.[3]

Here are some of their concerns: "[Donald Trump] uses fear to demonize and degrade immigrants, foreigners, and people from different racial, ethnic, and religious backgrounds.... [He] has fueled white American nationalism with xenophobic appeals and religious intolerance at the expense of gospel values.... We see this election as a significant teachable moment for our churches and our nation to bring about long-needed repentance from our racial sin."[4]

These evangelical leaders had the courage to speak truth to power, but most evangelical voters refused to heed their warning.[5]

---

2 Michael Gerson, "Trump Evangelicals Have Sold Their Souls," 12 March 2018, washingtonpost.com.
3 Colbert I. King, "In the Age of Trump, What Is a Christian?" 18 November 2016, washingtonpost.com.
4 https://www.change.org/p/donald-trump-a-declaration-by-american-evangelicals-concerning-donald-trump.
5 Jessica Martínez and Gregory A. Smith, "How the Faithful Voted: A Preliminary 2016 Analysis," 9 November 2016, pewresearch.org.

MEDITATION 22

When you stretch out your hands, I will hide my eyes from you;
even though you make many prayers, I will not listen;
your hands are full of blood.
Wash yourselves; make yourselves clean;
remove the evil of your doings from before my eyes;
cease to do evil, learn to do good;
seek justice, rescue the oppressed, defend the orphan,
plead for the widow.

—ISAIAH 1:15–17

MOST OF ISRAEL'S PROPHETS UTTERED GRIM WARNINGS LIKE THIS one. They reiterated the same basic message because their audiences clung the same core misconception. People had convinced themselves that participating in worship somehow excused them from complying with the moral demands of Scripture. The prophets, however, rejected that notion. They stressed, repeatedly, that observing religious rituals could never replace advancing social justice.

According to Isaiah, the deity would no longer listen to the people's prayers because their hands were "full of blood." Were all these people directly engaged in personal violence against their neighbors? No, of course not; but they were deeply complicit in the injustices of their society. Therefore, the deity viewed their indifference to the needs of the poor and their exploitation of the vulnerable as the moral equivalent of murder.

Members of the Religious Right, too, need constant reminders about such matters. How many times have they prayed for the poor in church and then gone home and grumbled about social welfare programs designed to help those very people? How many times have they prayed for the poor on Sunday and then gone to the polls on Tuesday and voted for candidates who promised to slash the funding for such programs?

Listen to the strident campaign rhetoric of politicians supported by the Religious Right nowadays. One might think from listening to their stump speeches that the only moral issues about which good Christian folks ought to be concerned involved policing what other people do in the privacy of their bedrooms. One would never guess that the moral issues about which the biblical prophets most often spoke involved caring for society's most vulnerable.

In the 2020 election, after having witnessed four years of Donald Trump's callous disregard for the needs of the poor, 85% of white evangelicals who attended church regularly and 63% of white Catholics who attended church regularly voted to give him four more years in office.[1] Most Sundays, those people took part in public worship and presumably offered their prayers in the name of Jesus. Thankfully, though, the deity was not listening.

---

1 Justin Nortey, "Most White Americans Who Regularly Attend Worship Service Voted for Trump in 2020," 30 August 2021, pewresearch. org.

MEDITATION 23

But strive first for the kingdom of God and his righteousness,
and all these things will be given to you as well.

—MATTHEW 6:33

THESE WORDS COME FROM A PASSAGE IN THE SERMON ON THE
Mount in which Jesus talks about what is most important. He
draws a sharp contrast between two vastly different lifestyles,
and his message remains just as relevant to Christians in
twenty-first century America as it was to his original audience
in first-century Palestine. Jesus urges his followers to adopt
a new way of life, one that radically reorders their priorities.

But what does Jesus mean by "the kingdom of God"?
Some churchgoers assume that he is referring to a spiritual
realm where the faithful go after death; yet that has nothing
to do with his thrust here. The familiar words of the Lord's
Prayer provide a better insight into his true concern: "Thy
kingdom come, thy will be done, on earth...." (Mt 6:10).
Simply put, seeking God's kingdom means doing God's will,
in the here and now.

According to Jesus, worries about material needs like
food and clothing should not be his followers' highest prior-
ity (Mt 6:25–32). He urges them, instead, to concern themselves with discerning the deity's will and devoting their efforts to doing that. Jesus is not suggesting that none of those
other things matter; he is simply saying that none of those
things should matter most. He urges his followers to embrace different values.

Writing in *The Atlantic*, Michael Gerson criticized the
political loyalty of the Religious Right: "Trump supporters

tend to dismiss moral scruples about his behavior as squeamishness over the president's 'style.' But the problem is the distinctly non-Christian substance of his *values*. Trump's unapologetic materialism—his equation of financial and social success with human achievement and worth—is a negation of Christian teaching."[1]

Peter Wehner expressed similar sentiments in an *Atlantic* article two years later: "A man whose lifestyle is more closely aligned with hedonism than with Christianity, Trump clearly sees white evangelicals as a means to an end, people to be used, suckers to be played." "In fact," Wehner added, "it's hard to imagine a person who has less affinity for...the teachings of Jesus...than Donald Trump."[2]

Gerson and Wehner have exposed the source of the Religious Right's moral bankruptcy. Trump's popularity with conservative white Christians undoubtedly rests on his ability to reflect their true values. Their professions of faith notwithstanding, these people have no interest whatsoever in seeking the kingdom of God. They are hellbent on pursuing a bigoted version of the American dream, one that excludes anyone who does not look like them.

---

1 Michael Gerson, "The Last Temptation," April 2018, theatlantic.com (emphasis original).
2 Peter Wehner, "Evangelicals Made a Bad Bargain with Trump," 18 October 2020, theatlantic.com.

MEDITATION 24

For what will it profit them if they gain
the whole world but forfeit their life?
Or what will they give in return for their life?

—MATTHEW 16:26

THE TRANSLATION "LIFE" OBSCURES THE ORIGINAL CONNOTATIONS of the Greek word *psyché*, which the King James Version aptly translated as "soul." The English word *soul*, like its Greek counterpart, denotes the spiritual part of a human being that comprises his or her personal identity and moral character. Thus, a better translation of Jesus' question would be, "For what will it profit them if they gain the whole world but forfeit their soul?"

In 2015, Texas governor Rick Perry issued a grave warning. "The White House has been occupied by giants," he said. "But from time to time, it is sought by the small-minded—divisive figures propelled by anger and appealing to the worst instincts of the human condition." He went on to describe the Trump campaign as "a toxic mix of demagoguery, mean-spiritedness, and nonsense" as well as "a cancer on conservatism."[1]

During the remainder of the 2016 campaign, Trump repeatedly confirmed Perry's worst fears. Yet shortly after that small-minded, mean-spirited demagogue took the oath of office as America's forty-fifth president, Perry joined the Trump administration as Secretary of Energy. In exchange for high office, he forfeited his integrity. As predicted, the malignancy metastasized, and he himself became one of its victims.[2]

1   Zeke J. Miller, "Rick Perry Calls Trump a Cancer and Carnival Act," 22 July 2015, time.com.
2   Maggie Haberman and Lisa Friedman, "Perry to Resign as Energy Secretary," 17 October 2019, nytimes.com.

Best-sellers by political pundits have documented numerous examples of other public officials and religious leaders who made comparable Faustian bargains in exchange for access to the Oval Office. However, prominent individuals were not the only ones who succumbed to that temptation. Millions of rank-and-file churchgoers convinced themselves that accepting moral trade-offs had always been the cost of doing business in Washington.

Consider opposition to abortion, the one issue concerning which members of the Religious Right could claim that Trump had upheld their belief. As noted earlier, that belief is grounded in a broader biblical ethic that includes concern for all of society's poor and vulnerable, because they too reflect the divine image. Yet, other than appointing Supreme Court justices committed to overturning *Roe v. Wade*, Trump has cruelly betrayed that ethic.

Stephanie Ranade Krider, former vice president and executive director of Ohio Right to Life, decried that glaring contradiction. In a *Washington Post* op-ed, Krider maintained that the pro-life movement's decision to align itself with Trump was a grave mistake. Single-issue voting on abortion, she argued, had made conservative Christians complicit in a range of other social policies that defied the teaching and example of Jesus.

Krider wrote, "Unfortunately, by endorsing Trump and defending him at every turn, our movement has placed power ahead of all else." Then, clearly alluding to Matthew 16:26, she offered this final assessment, "I am confident that, in advocating for this president, we [have] lost our soul. The church is meant to be known for our unconditional love of others. By supporting Trump, we show only our love of power."[3]

---

3   Stephanie Ranade Krider, "I'm a Pro-Life Evangelical. In Supporting Trump, My Movement Sold Its Soul," 8 October 2020, washingtonpost.com.

EPILOGUE

ON AUGUST 28, 1963, MARTIN LUTHER KING ADDRESSED A crowd of over 250,000 people from the steps of the Lincoln Memorial. He contrasted America's unfulfilled promise of human equality with his own vision of a more perfect union—one that he evoked with the stirring refrain, "I have a dream." Perhaps the most personal and poignant possibility that he imagined was this: "I have a dream that my four little children will one day live in a nation where they will not be judged by the color of their skin but by the content of their character."[1] That statement remains etched in this nation's consciousness, though few Americans have appreciated its full import. Those who cite it often do so only to decry the continuing injustice of racial discrimination, while ignoring King's belief that there is a legitimate benchmark by which to judge people: the content of their character. An immutable trait like skin color says nothing determinative about a person, but the desires and dispositions that one has deliberately cultivated and routinely displayed speak volumes.

Donald Trump has never left any doubt about the content of his character. Long before he entered the political arena, his pattern of racial bigotry had proved him unfit for public service.[2] After he announced his run for the presidency, Republican leaders initially repudiated Trump, hoping to pre-

1 Martin Luther King, Jr., *I Have a Dream: Writings and Speeches that Changed the World*, edited by James Melvin Washington (New York: Harper, 1992), 104.
2 Nicholas Kristof, "Is Donald Trump a Racist?" 23 July 2016, nytimes. com.

49

vent him from becoming the party standard bearer. Trump, though, grasped what his critics did not, the blind devotion of his supporters. At an Iowa campaign rally, he boasted, "I could stand in the middle of 5th Avenue and shoot somebody and I wouldn't lose voters."[3] Then, just four weeks before the 2016 election, the *Washington Post* published the *Access Hollywood* tape in which Trump bragged about sexually assaulting women.[4] In both cases, his words betrayed the content of his character. Yet, when Americans cast their ballots, sixty-two million voters,[5] as predicted, did likewise. Sadly, that number included 81% of white evangelicals and 60% of white Catholics.[6]

Journalists have now published well-sourced books detailing Trump's character flaws: his childish narcissism, petty cruelty, willful ignorance, reckless incompetence, and utter disdain for the truth—in short, his fundamental indecency. Of course, others share responsibility for his heedless mistakes and presumptuous misconduct while in office. Elected officials and political appointees alike violated their oath to support the constitution, and instead genuflected to a man who invariably put his own selfish interests above the common good. Nonetheless, the primary responsibility for the crisis confronting America today falls upon the tens of millions of white Christians who manifest this nation's worst impulses and inclinations. The problem is neither these people's political party nor their religious affiliation. The problem is the content of their character. Good people disagree

---

3   Jeremy Diamond, "Trump: I Could 'Shoot Somebody and I Wouldn't Lose Voters,'" 24 January 2016, cnn.com.
4   David A. Fahrenthold, "Trump Recorded Having Extremely Lewd Conversation about Women in 2005," 8 October 2016, washingtonpost.com.
5   "Presidential Election Results," 9 November 2016, nytimes.com.
6   Jessica Martínez and Gregory A. Smith, "How the Faithful Voted: A Preliminary 2016 Analysis," 9 November 2016, pewresearch.org.

about social, economic, and political issues; honest differences of opinion remain inevitable. Nonetheless, the members of the Religious Right who continue to embrace the deranged delusions of a blustering bully are not good people.

Writer Isabel Wilkerson has shed new light on the crucial role that caste plays in uniting such people. What she clarifies about Trump voters in general undoubtedly holds true for the millions of white evangelicals and white Catholics who have now cast ballots for him twice. By supporting Trump, Wilkerson explains, these people are not voting against their interests; they are voting "to preserve what their actions say they value most—the benefits they had grown accustomed to as members of the historically ruling class in America."[7] Wilkerson's analysis confirms the findings of Randall Balmer: "There is a kind of tragic continuity in the Religious Right's embrace of Donald Trump. A movement that began with the defense of racial segregation in the late 1970s climbed into bed with a vulgar demagogue who recognizes 'some good people' among white supremacists, who equivocates about denouncing a representative of the Ku Klux Klan, and who admonished a white supremacist terrorist group to 'stand by' in advance of the 2020 election."[8] The basic problem, undoubtedly, is the content of these people's character.

The Bible condemns those who honor God with their lips but whose hearts are far from him (Isa 29:13; Mk 7:6). It teaches that humankind is created in the divine image (Gen 1:27) and that people are to love their neighbors as themselves (Lev 19:18; Mk 12:31). The Bible prohibits bearing false witness (Ex 20:16) and denounces those who call

---

7 Isabel Wilkerson, *Caste: The Origins of Our Discontents* (New York: Random House, 2020), 325.
8 Randall Balmer, *Bad Faith: Race and the Rise of the Religious Right* (Grand Rapids: Eerdmans, 2021), 78.

evil good (Isa 5:20). It teaches that people should defend the most vulnerable members of society: the widow, the orphan, the poor, and the alien (Isa 1:17; Zech 7:10). Jesus repudiates those who call him Lord and yet fail to do God's will (Mt 7:21). He condemns those who fail to feed the hungry, welcome the stranger, or care for the sick and imprisoned (Mt 25:41–43). Jesus teaches that no one can serve two masters (Mt 6:24); however, that is exactly what an unholy alliance of white evangelicals and white Catholics has tried to do. They have abandoned their calling to follow Jesus (Mk 8:34) and, instead, put their faith in the empty promises of a contemptible fool.

According to the Bible, repentance involves more than a feeling of remorse or regret; it requires a radical change of mind, one evidenced by a commensurate reordering of behavior. James Baldwin once said, "Not everything that is faced can be changed; but nothing can be changed until it is faced."[9] The members of the Religious Right desperately need to repent, but they must first face their apostasy.

---

9   James Baldwin, "As Much Truth as One Can Bear," 14 January 1962, nytimes.com.

SUGGESTIONS FOR FURTHER READING

Balmer, Randall
Bad Faith: Race and the Rise of the Religious Right. Grand Rapids: Eerdmans, 2021.

Crossan, John Dominic
God and Empire: Jesus Against Rome, Then and Now. New York: Harper, 2007.

Du Mez, Kristen-Kobes
Jesus and John Wayne: How White Evangelicals Corrupted a Faith and Fractured a Nation. New York: Liveright, 2020.

Fea, John
Believe Me: The Evangelical Road to Donald Trump. Grand Rapids: Eerdmans, 2018.

Hannah-Jones, Nikole, Caitlin Roper, Ilena Silverman, and Jake Silverstein
The 1619 Project: A New Origin Story. New York: One World, 2021.

Jones, Robert P.
White Too Long: The Legacy of White Supremacy in American Christianity. New York: Simon & Schuster, 2020.

Marti, Gerardo
American Blindspot: Race, Class, Religion, and the Trump Presidency. New York: Rowman & Littlefield, 2020.

McGhee, Heather
The Sum of Us: What Racism Costs Everyone and How We Can Prosper Together. New York: One World, 2021.

Posner, Sarah
  Unholy: Why White Evangelicals Worship at the Altar of Donald Trump. New York: Random House, 2020.

Sider, Ronald J., ed.
  The Spiritual Danger of Donald Trump: 30 Evangelical Christians on Justice, Truth, and Moral Integrity. Eugene, OR: Cascade Books, 2020.

Stewart, Katherine
  The Power Worshipers: Inside the Dangerous Rise of Christian Nationalism. New York: Bloomsbury, 2019.

Wallis, Jim
  America's Original Sin: Racism, White Privilege, and a Bridge to a New America. Grand Rapids: Brazos, 2016.

Wilkerson, Isabel
  Caste: The Origins of Our Discontents. New York: Random House, 2020.

Zahnd, Brian
  Postcards from Babylon: The Church in American Exile. Jefferson City, MO: Spello Press, 2019.

ABOUT THE AUTHOR

GEORGE CHUMNEY is a retired Presbyterian minister. In addition to his pastoral duties in a handful of small-town churches, he has also worked as a middle school history teacher. He has a brilliant and beautiful wife, two wonderful children, and four delightful grandchildren. If you would like to schedule him to speak to your group or organization, please contact his publisher, Easty Lambert-Brown at borgogirl@ bellsouth.net.

CPSIA information can be obtained
at www.ICGtesting.com
Printed in the USA
LVHW051541130722
723348LV00011B/297